King Tut's Curse

King Tut, the ancient Egyptian king, was buried with a great deal of gold and many treasures. To protect his tomb from robbers, he placed a curse on it before he died. The curse was supposed to cause the death of anyone who opened his tomb.

No one tried to open it until thousands of years later, when an expedition of archaeologists discovered the tomb and unsealed it. Thirteen years later, twenty-one deaths were said to have been caused by the curse. Was it just coincidence? Or can a curse *kill?* . . .

FAMOUS CURSES

DANIEL COHEN

**Illustrated with photographs
and prints**

AN ARCHWAY PAPERBACK
Published by POCKET BOOKS • NEW YORK

The following illustrations are used by permission and through the courtesy of: Griffith Institute, Ashmolean Museum, 6, 8; from *The Great Orm of Loch Ness* by F. W. Holiday, W. W. Norton & Co., 31; Library of Congress, 81, 82, 83, 84; The Metropolitan Museum of Art, 10; National Gallery of Art, Washington, D.C., 12; New York Public Library Picture Collection, 39, 49, 51, 72, 74, 75, 87, 94, 95, 101, 102; from *Nineteenth-Century Stage* by Stanley Appelbaum, Dover Publications, Inc., 71; Radio Times Hulton Picture Library, 24; Smithsonian Institution Photo by Dane Alexander Penland, 38; UPI, 42, 105.

An Archway Paperback published by
POCKET BOOKS, a division of Simon & Schuster, Inc.
1230 Avenue of the Americas, New York, N.Y. 10020

Published by arrangement with Dodd, Mead & Company
Library of Congress Catalog Card Number: 79-52039

ISBN: 0-671-41867-X

First Pocket Books printing May, 1981

10 9 8 7 6 5 4 3 2

AN ARCHWAY PAPERBACK and colophon are
registered trademarks of Simon and Schuster, Inc.

Printed in the U.S.A.

IL 4+

For Shirley Shannon,
without whom this book,
and many others,
would not have been possible.

Contents

FAMOUS CURSES

INTRODUCTION

THE LIBRARIANS' CURSE

People have been cursing one another for thousands of years.

There were times when a curse could be very useful. Curses sometimes protected the weak from the strong. To be cursed by a beggar, a widow, or someone you had wronged was thought to be very dangerous. Evil people may have been restrained from doing more evil from fear of a curse.

Curses were used to protect things like tombs and jewels from robbers.

The dying tried to revenge themselves with a curse, or make sure that their wishes would be carried out after death. A deathbed curse was particularly feared.

So a curse, you can see, is not always evil.

In this book we are going to explore many types of curses, both good and evil. First, I would like to describe a type of curse that really was used five or six hundred years ago.

At that time all books were copied by hand. They were very expensive and very rare. Most books were kept in the libraries of monasteries. The monks in charge of these libraries would often attach a curse to the books. It called down all the powers of heaven to punish thieves and careless borrowers.

So be warned!

1

KING TUT'S CURSE

Did the kings of ancient Egypt protect their tombs with curses?

Did one of these curses reach across the centuries to cause the death of the people who had opened the tomb?

According to the legend of King Tut's curse, that is exactly what happened. It is the best-known curse story of modern times. You have probably heard it yourself. But is that what really happened? Let us take a closer look at King Tut and his curse.

King Tut, or really Tutankhamun, ruled Egypt about 3,500 years ago. He ruled for only a short time. By the age of nineteen he was dead. Perhaps he had been murdered, for he must have had many enemies.

Tutankhamun came to the throne of Egypt at a bad time. There was a great deal of political and religious unrest. Later kings tried to wipe out all memory of Tutankhamun. His name was taken out of the official king lists. His picture was hammered out of temple walls. His enemies tried to make the world forget that Tutankhamun had ever existed. Without knowing it, his enemies may have done him a favor. Today Tutankhamun is the best known of all the kings of ancient Egypt.

The ancient Egyptians buried their kings with a great deal of gold and many other treasures. This made the tombs of the kings rich

4

prizes for robbers. Over the centuries every royal tomb in Egypt was robbed. Every tomb, that is, except the tomb of King Tutankhamun. He was almost completely forgotten. The robbers may just have overlooked his tomb.

Tutankhamun's enemies had not completely wiped out all trace of him. His name was known to a few archaeologists. Archaeologists are scientists who study how people lived in ancient times. The scientists could find no record that Tutankhamun's tomb had ever been found by robbers. There was a slim hope that his tomb might still be found.

One of those who held such a hope was an Englishman named Howard Carter. Carter had come to Egypt in 1891, when he was only seventeen years old. He spent years working for other archaeologists. He came to believe that he could find the lost tomb. Carter had no money of his own, and digging in Egypt was expensive.

Carter teamed up with Lord Carnarvon, a very rich Englishman who had an interest in Egypt. Carter supervised most of the digging while Carnarvon supplied all of the money. Carnarvon, however, did spend a good deal of time in Egypt helping Carter.

Howard Carter was sure that Tutankhamun's tomb was to be found in the Valley of the Kings. That was a burial place for many of the kings of Tutankhamun's time. He began

Howard Carter (left) and associate Arthur C. Mace, opening a sealed door in the tomb.

digging in the Valley in 1914. For years the expeditions found little or nothing. By the start of 1922 Lord Carnarvon had become discouraged, and decided to stop paying for expeditions. Carter knew it was to be his last season of digging in the Valley.

On November 4, 1922, Carter's workmen uncovered a step cut into the rock. Working carefully, they found sixteen steps and at the end a sealed doorway. The doorway contained the name Tutankhamun. Whatever was behind that door had not been touched by robbers.

Carter sent a telegram to Carnarvon at once:

AT LAST HAVE MADE A WONDERFUL DISCOVERY IN VALLEY. MAGNIFICENT TOMB WITH SEALS INTACT. RECOVERED SAME FOR YOUR ARRIVAL. CONGRATULATIONS.

Carnarvon rushed back to Egypt.

On November 26, 1922, the diggers reached another sealed door. Carter made a small hole in it. His hands were shaking so badly he could barely hold the candle he needed for light. He peered into the hole, but could say nothing. Carnarvon, who was standing behind him, became impatient and asked if he saw anything. Carter said, "Yes, wonderful things!"

Later he said, "As my eyes grew accustomed to the light, details of the room within emerged slowly from the mist, strange animals,

Howard Carter opens the shrine which held the mummy
of King Tutankhamun.

statues, and gold—everywhere the glint of gold."

By now Carnarvon was pulling at Carter's arm shouting, "Here, let me have a look." Finally Carter was pulled away from the hole and, when Carnarvon took his place, he too was amazed. Soon the whole world was to be amazed.

What Howard Carter and Lord Carnarvon had found was the tomb of King Tutankhamun completely undisturbed. It was just as it had been when the king's mummy was sealed up in it 3,500 years earlier. Tutankhamun had been a minor king. Still, he had been buried with hundreds of beautifully made objects and thousands of pounds of gold. One of the three coffins enclosing the mummy was made from 2,500 pounds of pure gold.

When the discovery became known it made headlines all over the world. People who had never heard of Tutankhamun and knew little or nothing of ancient Egypt were fascinated. The fascination continues to this day. During the 1970s a small number of objects from King Tut's tomb have been exhibited in different cities around the world. People still stand in line for hours just to get a glimpse at the marvelous objects.

That is the wonder of Tutankhamun, but what about the curse? Stories of a curse started almost as soon as the tomb was discovered.

Solid gold funeral mask of King Tutankhamun

Ancient Egypt has always had a reputation for the supernatural. It is one of the oldest civilizations in the world. Even other ancient people thought the Egyptians had magical secrets.

Tombs—any kind of tombs—are spooky. Egyptian tombs are especially spooky because they contain mummies. Mummies are dried and preserved bodies. Egyptian mummies are wrapped in linen cloth. A well-preserved body that is thousands of years old makes most people feel creepy.

According to the legend, the first victim of the curse was Howard Carter's canary. Carter was very fond of his pet bird. A few days after the discovery of the tomb the bird was killed by a cobra. The cobra is one of the symbols of ancient Egyptian royalty.

The second victim was a more serious one— Lord Carnarvon himself. In March, 1923, Carnarvon became ill. He was taken to the hospital in Cairo. On April 5, he was dead. It was less than half a year after he first entered the tomb of King Tutankhamun. The cause of his death is not really known. He seems to have gotten an infection, perhaps from an insect bite.

Carnarvon was only fifty-seven years old when he died. But he had not been a healthy man for years. Twenty years earlier he had been in a serious automobile accident. He nearly died then. Afterward, he never fully

Gold charm from King Tut's tomb

recovered. It was because of his poor health that he took up archaeology as a hobby. Still, his sudden death was completely unexpected.

At the exact moment of Carnarvon's death something strange happened in Cairo. All the lights in the city went out briefly. An investigation was begun, but the cause of the blackout could never be discovered. A lot of people thought it was connected with the death of Lord Carnarvon and the curse of King Tut.

Back in England at Lord Carnarvon's estate,

one of his favorite dogs began to howl. It then fell over dead, at about the same moment its master died in faraway Egypt.

Carnarvon's death created almost as much of a sensation as finding the tomb. The legend of the Curse of King Tut was well launched. Every time someone who had been connected with King Tut's tomb died, some people said the curse had struck again. By 1929 eleven people associated with the Tutankhamun tomb were dead. Among them were Carnarvon's half brother, and another relative, Lady Elizabeth Carnarvon. Astonishingly, she too died of an infected insect bite.

Carter's personal secretary, Richard Bethell, was found dead in his chair at his fashionable London club. The cause of his death was never determined, or if it was, was never made public. A short time later Bethell's father, Lord Westbury, jumped to his death from a building near Buckingham Palace. Lord Westbury left behind a note which said: "I really cannot stand any more horrors and I hardly see what good I am going to do here, so I am going to make my exit." The hearse carrying Lord Westbury's body knocked down and killed an eight-year-old boy.

In the following years there were more deaths attributed to the curse. By 1935 the total number of curse "victims" was supposed to have reached twenty-one.

But now we must ask what may seem like a silly question: Was there a curse on King Tut's tomb in the first place? Many stories say that the curse was carved above the door to the tomb. It read:

DEATH SHALL COME ON SWIFT WINGS TO HIM WHO DISTURBS THE PEACE OF THE KING

Unfortunately for the legend, there is no such carving in the tomb. Other versions of the legend say that the curse was found on a stone tablet in the tomb. According to this version, the tablet was hidden away. It was said that Carter thought his workmen might refuse to dig in a cursed tomb. Later, according to this story, the tablet was lost. But there is no record of any such tablet ever being found. Nor is there any other evidence of such a find.

Besides, the whole idea of a cursed tomb is very un-Egyptian. Many other ancient people did place curses on those who disturbed the graves of their dead. Some not so ancient people did too.

The great dramatist William Shakespeare had this curse carved on his tombstone:

Blest be the man that spares these stones
Cursed be he that moves my bones.

But of all of the thousands of tombs found in Egypt, only two contained curses of any kind. One of them found on the mummy case of a high priest read: "May the cobra on my head spit flames of fire into thy face, and may thy head be in the place of my feet."

Despite this, cursed tombs were practically unknown in Egypt. There is no reason to believe that King Tut's tomb was any different.

If there was no supernatural curse on the tomb, is it possible that something else happened? People pointed out that the tomb had been completely sealed for over 3,000 years. They said that some sort of germ or poison, unknown to the modern world, was sealed up inside. Those who first entered the tomb might have been affected by it.

When Carter and Carnarvon first opened the tomb they knew there might be hidden dangers. They had the air and the contents of the tomb tested thoroughly. Nothing harmful was found.

Well, then, how do we explain all of those strange deaths?

There is no doubt that the death of Lord Carnarvon was both strange and tragic. So were some of the other deaths blamed on the curse. But a lot of people were connected in one way or another with finding the tomb. Most of them lived out perfectly normal lives. The best example is Howard Carter himself. More than anyone else, he was responsible for finding and opening the tomb. Yet he did not die until 1939, when he was sixty-six years old. That was almost seventeen years after the opening of the tomb. If Carter's death was due to a curse, death did not exactly come on "swift wings." Carter died only after he had finished all of his work on the Tutankhamun tomb.

Lord Carnarvon's son and daughter were both with their father in Egypt. In 1970 a reporter found both of them alive and in excellent health, though one was in her seventies and the other in his eighties.

Howard Carter didn't believe in any curse. He thought that anyone who did was foolish. No other professional archaeologist believes in the curse either. One said that if Egyptian tombs were cursed, then all the archaeologists would be dead. Flinders Petrie, who was one of the greatest archaeologists ever to work in Egypt, and Howard Carter's first teacher, lived to be ninety-two. Petrie had visited Tutankhamun's tomb, and most other tombs in Egypt as well.

Sometimes people do die unexpectedly, just as Lord Carnarvon did.

Sometimes people become so depressed and unhappy that they kill themselves, just as Lord Westbury did.

If such things happen to ordinary people, we might say, "How terrible, how tragic!" When such things happen to people who were somehow connected with ancient Egyptian tombs, we might say, "The curse got them."

The story of King Tut's curse really has no evidence to support it. But the idea is too exciting to give up. It will probably be repeated for as long as people are interested in King Tut. And that will probably be a very, very long time.

2
THE CRAWLS

The Tichborne family is one of the oldest in Britain. Records of the family go back over 1,000 years. They were very rich and owned a lot of land in the area called Hampshire.

The story of the Tichborne curse starts in the twelfth century, about 800 years ago. Roger de Tichborne, son of the head of the family, married Lady Mabella de Lymerston. They were a badly matched pair.

Roger was a tough, often violent soldier. He spent most of his time away from home, fighting in one war or the other. He cared little or nothing for religion or for the welfare of the people who lived on his lands.

Lady Mabella, on the other hand, was very sensitive and devoutly religious. She was deeply moved by the awful conditions in which the common folk lived. Lady Mabella spent her time trying to help the poor.

Even as she lay dying she did not forget the poor. She begged her husband to set aside part of his land to provide an annual distribution of bread and flour to the poor. Roger treated the request with scorn. He made her an offer. He said that he would gladly set aside all of the land that she could encircle while carrying a blazing torch. Since Lady Mabella was so weak that no one thought she could even rise from her bed, the offer was not a serious one.

Roger had not reckoned on his wife's iron

will. She lit a torch from the fireplace. She asked her servants to carry her to the open land. Lady Mabella then proceeded to crawl in a wide circle. The strength of the dying woman seemed almost supernatural. Before the torch finally went out, she had encircled twenty-three acres of land.

Lady Mabella still did not trust her husband to keep his word. So she backed up her actions by placing a curse on the family. If Roger or his heirs failed to provide the bread and flour for the poor, the family would die out. Seven ill-fated sons would be born, followed by a generation of seven daughters. The house would fall down. Then the ancient family name would be extinct.

Roger de Tichborne granted his dying wife's request. The distribution of bread and flour was to be made on Lady Day. That was a day for special prayers to the Virgin Mary. Lady Mabella had always been devoted to the Virgin.

Roger also made special provision in his will to set aside the twenty-three acres for the poor. To this day the area is still known as "The Crawls."

Roger and his heirs were faithful to the promise. For centuries bread and flour were distributed by the family on Lady Day. The custom became known as the Tichborne Dole. A dole is giving something to the needy.

Unfortunately, the free bread attracted more than the local poor. People from all over used to visit the area to get bread. Many of these people were criminals. The crowds also became hard to handle. In 1794 the crowd that gathered for the Tichborne Dole nearly staged a riot. To avoid further trouble the local government banned the Dole altogether.

At that time the head of the family was Sir Henry Tichborne. He had seven sons—Henry, Benjamin, Edward, James, John, George, and Roger. The bad luck for the family began in 1802, eight years after the Dole stopped. George died. A short time later part of the ancient Tichborne house actually did fall down. The rest of the house was demolished because it was unsafe.

In 1806—four years later—John, the fifth son, died in the East Indies. Four years after that Benjamin, the second son, died in China. Neither son had married. Roger, the youngest son, did marry but died childless. Henry, the eldest of the Tichborne sons, also married and had seven daughters, but no son.

Perhaps in an attempt to escape the curse, the third son Edward changed his name to Doughty. He married and had one son, Henry, who died in 1836 at the age of six. That tragedy was too much for Edward. He ordered that the Dole be started again. It has continued until this day.

That still leaves one of the sons to be accounted for—James. He had married in 1827 and had two sons. The first, Roger Charles Tichborne, was born before the Dole had been restored. The second, Albert Joseph, was born afterward.

Of all the ancient Tichborne family, Roger, who bore the name of Lady Mabella's husband, may have had the strangest fate. In 1853 Roger Tichborne sailed to South America. He stayed there for several months and then set sail for Jamaica. The ship on which he was traveling never arrived at Jamaica.

Almost everyone assumed that the ship had sunk and Roger had drowned. But his mother was not sure. She advertised in newspapers around the world for news of her missing son. In 1865 a man from Australia appeared, who said he really was the missing Roger. This man became known as the Tichborne Claimant. A claimant is a person who claims something. This man claimed to be Roger Tichborne. The Claimant said that he had been living in South America and Australia.

This story was accepted by Lady Tichborne and some of the missing Roger's friends. However, most thought that the man called the Claimant was a fraud who wanted Roger's money. Roger's younger brother, Alfred Joseph, sued the Claimant. The case dragged on in the courts for years. Finally the Claimant

The Tichborne Claimant

was completely defeated. He was sent to prison for fourteen years. But through it all the Claimant continued to insist that he was the missing Roger.

The Claimant probably was a fraud. He didn't know many things that Roger Tichborne should have known. There was evidence produced that he was really Arthur Orton, a butcher's son. But there is something to be said for the other side as well. We can't be absolutely sure whether the Claimant was one of the greatest frauds of all times, or a very unfortunate Roger Tichborne.

All in all, the case was a disaster for the family. The Tichborne fortune was practically ruined by the legal costs. The family, however, did continue. Sir Anthony Doughty-Tichborne was the last man to hold the title. His only son died shortly after his birth. Sir Anthony himself died in 1968. The ancient Tichborne name is now extinct.

The Tichborne Dole, however, is still carried on. It is now administered by the Church. Once a year flour is distributed to local villagers at 3:00 P.M. on Lady Day, March 25. Before it is distributed a priest blesses the flour. The ceremony ends with a prayer for the soul of Lady Mabella, whose charity—and curse—were responsible for the Dole in the first place.

3

THE LAMBTON
WORM

We may not like the way a worm looks, but we are not afraid of one. However, a few hundred years ago in England the word "worm" had a different meaning. It was not a little wiggly thing that comes out of the ground—it was a dragon.

There is a very strange old English tale about that kind of worm and what it did to a family named Lambton that lived in the county of Durham.

The story began about 1420. Young John Lambton, heir to the family estates, was not very religious. He spent his Sundays fishing in the River Wear, rather than going to church. This was a great scandal to the church-going members of the community. They thought it would lead to no good. It turned out they were right.

One Sunday young Lambton hooked something very lively. A stranger asked him what he had caught, and Lambton replied, "Why, truly, I think I've caught the Devil." He finally did pull in his catch, after a great struggle. It wasn't the Devil, but it wasn't an ordinary fish either. It was a disgusting-looking worm. Lambton didn't want to keep the ugly thing. But he didn't want to throw it back in the river either. So he threw it down a well. Later, the place came to be known as Worm Well.

The creature liked the well and grew quickly.

When it was large enough, it got out of the well and went back to the river. The Worm could often be seen sunning itself on a rock in the middle of the river. It also came ashore. Its favorite spot was a large mound now known as Worm Hill.

Young John Lambton knew none of this. He had given up his easy-going life and joined the Crusades. He spent years fighting in the Holy Land. When he finally returned to County Durham he found a very serious situation.

The Worm was now huge. It was roaming the countryside. People were afraid to go out to work their fields. His own father, Lord Lambton, was practically a prisoner in his castle. There had been several unsuccessful attempts to kill the Worm. But the monster had the power to reunite whatever part of its body had been cut off. Those who tried to kill the Worm were themselves killed.

John Lambton decided that since he was responsible for the Worm, he had better get rid of it. But he knew he needed help, so he went to a local witch for advice.

She told him that he must wear armor covered with pointed spear blades, and that he must trust his sword. If he did kill the Worm, he had to vow also to kill the next living thing he saw. If he did not, the witch said, then no Lord Lambton, for the next nine generations, would die in bed.

The witch's curse was a powerful one, but John Lambton had a plan. If he killed the Worm he would blow his hunting horn. That would be a signal for the people at the castle to release a hound. John Lambton would kill the dog to fulfill his vow.

Lambton then went out to the Worm's favorite rock and waited for it. He didn't have to wait long. The Worm quickly appeared out of the water and tried to strangle Lambton in its coils. But it was pierced by the spear blades in the armor. The Worm became so weak from its wounds that Lambton was able to hack it in two with his sword. One half of the Worm was then caught in the swift-moving river current and swept away. The Worm, unable to reunite itself, died.

John Lambton's triumph was complete. He blew on his hunting horn as planned. But then something went wrong. Back at the castle old Lord Lambton was so relieved when he heard the horn that he forgot the plan and went rushing out to greet his son. He was the first living thing that John Lambton saw after killing the Worm.

John Lambton could not kill his father to fulfill the vow. So the curse descended upon the Lambton family.

Whether nine full generations of Lord Lambtons died violently is not certain. Quite a number of them did, however. John Lambton's son

Statue of Sir John Lambton
killing the Lambton Worm

Spiked armor was often used for fighting dragons.

Robert was drowned. Sir William Lambton was killed in battle, and so was his son. Others were also rumored to have met untimely ends. The ninth descending generation from the original Sir John was Henry Lambton. He was a member of the British parliament. He died, apparently from natural causes, while riding across a bridge. The curse seems to have ended with him.

The legend is still very popular today. And, as with all legends, it is sometimes a bit confused. There was a sword kept in the Cathedral library at Durham. It was a very old curved sword. Visitors were told that this was the sword with which Sir John de Conyers killed the Worm of Sockburn. Sometime after 1865 the sword seems to have been lost.

What does the Lambton Worm have to do with the Worm of Sockburn? No one appears to know. Both legends seem to have started in the same general area, at about the same time. Perhaps both refer to the same event, or perhaps there were two Worms.

The Lambton family is still the one most closely connected with the Worm legend. You can go to County Durham and find Worm Rock and Worm Hill. The hill now has a war memorial on top of it. Not long ago I met a young Englishwoman who remembers taking part in a play about the Lambton Worm when

she was in school. She also sang me a very
long song about the Lambton Worm.

People who are interested in the Loch Ness
monster have also shown an interest in the
Lambton Worm. Some say that the Worm was
not a dragon, but something like the monster
that lives in Loch Ness.

There is no way of proving that theory either
true or false. Like so many other legends, the
origins of the legend of the Lambton Worm are
lost forever. We may believe what we wish
about it.

4

THE DIAMOND OF DOOM

How would you like to own one of the largest and most perfect diamonds in the world? You would? Think again! This particular diamond has brought bad luck to an awful lot of people who did own it.

The diamond is the famous Hope Diamond. You can't own it but you can see it. The beautiful, sparkling, blue stone is now the property of the United States and is on display at the Smithsonian Institution in Washington. Every year thousands come to stare at it. It is not only the beauty of the stone, but its evil reputation that attracts the crowds.

Many famous gems are supposed to carry curses. Among them are the Great Mogul, the Orloff Diamond, the Moon of the Mountains, and the Kohinoor. But no curse is as famous as the curse of the Hope Diamond.

The legend of the Hope Diamond may have inspired the author Wilkie Collins to write *The Moonstone*. *The Moonstone* is considered the first mystery novel ever written. It is about a precious stone that brings bad luck and death to its owners. Cursed stones have appeared in many other works of fiction. But the Hope Diamond is very real.

What was to become the Hope Diamond first appears in history in the seventeenth century. A French trader named John Baptiste Tavernier brought from India a large, blue

112.50-carat diamond. Tavernier would not say how he got the diamond. There were rumors that he had stolen it from the eye of an idol, in the temple of Rama-Sita, near Mandalay. There was also a rumor that the god would revenge himself upon anyone who stole the diamond.

Still, it was a beautiful diamond, one fit for a king. And it was a king who bought it. King Louis XIV of France not only paid a huge sum of money for the diamond, he made Tavernier a baron as part of the deal. Neither the money nor the title did Tavernier much good. He lost his fortune and died while traveling through Russia.

Louis XIV had the diamond cut into a heart shape. It was then called the French Blue. The curse, if there was one, does not seem to have troubled Louis XIV. He was one of France's most powerful, and long-lived monarchs. Indeed, the story of the curse didn't really get started until the diamond passed into the hands of the king's grandson, King Louis XVI.

This king gave the diamond to his wife, Queen Marie Antoinette. Both the king and the queen had their reigns cut short and their heads cut off during the French Revolution. A close friend of the queen's, Princess de Lamballe, who had often borrowed the diamond to wear, was said to have been torn to pieces by an angry mob.

During the chaos of the French Revolution

The Hope Diamond

the diamond disappeared. It had been stolen,
and then recut. Part of it appeared rather mys-
teriously in London. The diamond, now re-
duced to 44.50 carats, was sold to a wealthy
banker, Henry Thomas Hope. It was from the
British banker that the diamond got the name
by which it is best known.

Fortunately for the banker, but unfortunately for the curse legend, Hope never seems
to have suffered any particular ill-fortune.
Hope never married, and on his death the diamond was inherited by other members of his

Marie Antoinette on her way to the guillotine

family. The only member of the family who seems to have suffered excessive bad luck was May Yohe, a singer who married Lord Francis Hope. She divorced Hope and ultimately died alone and in poverty in 1938. She always blamed the diamond for her bad luck.

But by that time she didn't have the diamond. The Hope family sold it in 1901. It went to two different jewelers. One was reported to have gone bankrupt, the other killed himself.

Probably the most dramatic victim of the curse was the diamond's next owner, a drunken Russian nobleman named Prince Kanitovski. The prince was madly in love with a French showgirl, much younger than himself. One night he allowed her to wear the diamond on stage. During the middle of the performance the prince stood up in the audience and shot the girl dead. No one knows why.

But that wasn't the end. According to some accounts of the legend, Prince Kanitovski was then stabbed to death by a group that called themselves Russian revolutionaries.

The diamond then passed into the hands of a Greek jeweler, who promptly fell off a cliff. Then it was purchased by another monarch, Sultan Abdul Hamid of Turkey.

Abdul Hamid was to be the last Sultan of Turkey. Although he didn't know it, he may have suspected it. His power was slipping away, and the Turkish empire was crumbling.

Several attempts were made on his life. He locked himself up in his palace, never going out in public. He always carried a gun in his pocket, and he shot several people by accident. One of them reportedly was the Sultana who was wearing the Hope Diamond at the time. The Sultan got the name, Abdul the Damned.

After Abdul Hamid was removed from his throne, the diamond turned up in the hands of a Persian dealer, who was drowned in an ocean liner disaster. It was then acquired by the famous French jeweler, Pierre Cartier. He in turn sold it to Edward B. McLean, heir to an American newspaper fortune, and his independently wealthy wife Evalyn. She was the daughter of a miner who had struck it rich.

Shortly after purchasing the diamond, McLean's mother died. So did two of the servants in the McLean household. Edward McLean himself seems to have been rather wary of the gem. But Evalyn McLean loved it and dismissed all talk of a curse as nonsense. She often wore the diamond, now set in a necklace.

There were other deaths in the McLean family. By far the most tragic was the death of the McLeans' ten-year-old son Vinson. He ran out in front of the family home in Washington, D.C., and was killed by a car. The boy had been called the $100 million baby, because of the huge amount of money he was to inherit,

Evalyn McLean wearing the Hope Diamond

if he had lived. Usually he was carefully guarded. His mother was afraid that he would be kidnapped. One of the few times he slipped away from strict supervision he was killed.

The McLean marriage had never been a very happy one. The main reason was that Edward McLean was a heavy drinker. The marriage finally ended in divorce. This shattered McLean's fragile mental stability. He was committed to a mental institution where he finally died.

Still, Evalyn McLean refused to part with the diamond. But she did offer to give it up once. In 1932 the young son of the famous aviator Charles Lindbergh was kidnapped. Mrs. McLean used the diamond to try and raise money for the boy's ransom. But the man who was supposed to be collecting the money was a crook. Mrs. McLean had to raise more money to get her diamond back. The Lindbergh child was found dead.

In 1946 the McLeans' only daughter died suddenly. She had accidentally taken too many sleeping pills. Some people remembered that at her wedding, five years earlier, she had worn the Hope Diamond.

The next year Evalyn McLean herself died. She was old and there was nothing unusual about her death. To the end, she firmly rejected any idea of a curse.

Two years after her death many of the

McLean gems, including the Hope Diamond, were purchased by the famous New York jeweler, Harry Winston. The price for all the gems was $1 million.

The jeweler put the Hope Diamond on display in New York and other places for years. Then he decided to donate it to the nation. Winston took the diamond, then estimated to be worth about $1 million, to the post office. He sent it by ordinary parcel post to the Smithsonian Institution in Washington, D.C. He paid about $150 for insurance on the package, but otherwise took no extra precautions. Many of us are afraid that our ordinary letters will not arrive safely. But Harry Winston said that he had no second thoughts about sending one of the most valuable diamonds in the world through the mail.

The package arrived safely. The great blue diamond is now one of the most popular exhibits in the Smithsonian. Exhibited along with the diamond is the package in which it was sent. Some people joke that perhaps the diamond has cursed the postal service. That is why mail delivery is so expensive, and often so poor.

More seriously, some believers in the curse remind you that the president is technically custodian of the Hope Diamond. They point to the assassination of John F. Kennedy and the disgrace and resignation of Richard M. Nixon as examples of more bad luck from the curse.

Does the Hope Diamond really bring bad luck? Is it somehow cursed? The list of disasters that have befallen those who owned the diamond is impressive. But we often forget that many of those who owned the diamond—King Louis XIV, Henry Hope, whose name the diamond bears, Evalyn McLean, who had the diamond longer than anyone else in recent years, and Harry Winston, the diamond's last private owner—did not die untimely deaths.

Many people who never owned the Hope Diamond, or any other objects said to be cursed, have died suddenly or violently. And we are not really sure that all of the stories told about the Hope Diamond are true. The diamond changed hands many times. Sometimes buyers and sellers wished to keep the deal secret. False stories about who owned, or didn't own, the diamond were spread. Once the diamond got the reputation of being cursed, anything bad that happened to anyone remotely connected with the diamond was blamed on the curse.

So the story of the curse of the Hope Diamond has a lot of holes in it. But like the story of the curse of King Tut, it is too good to give up.

5

THE KNIGHTS OF
THE TEMPLE

The Knights of the Temple, or the Templars, were a strange group. And they met a strange fate.

The group was begun around the year 1188 by a very religious French knight named Hugh de Payens and about eight of his friends. They vowed to dedicate their lives to protecting Christians who wanted to visit the Holy Land.

Many knights fired by religious feelings joined, and the group grew rapidly. Many wealthy nobles who did not join gave the knights property and money.

The once-small band of companions was soon organized along formal lines. They had to live by very strict rules. Each member cut his hair short, but let his beard grow long. Their uniform was a white cloak decorated with a large red cross. They vowed never to marry. Indeed, they avoided women entirely.

Individual knights were allowed to own nothing except their own clothes and weapons. The group itself, however, grew rich from the many gifts showered upon it. In later years the wealth was to cause them great grief.

Another rule of the group was obedience. They were to obey the orders of the leader of the group, who was called the Grand Master, absolutely and without question. The first Grand Master was Hugh de Payens. This rule, too, was to come back to haunt them.

A Templar

But perhaps the most troublesome rule of all was the rule of secrecy. When any member joined the group he had to undergo an initiation ceremony. He had to swear never to reveal the details of that ceremony or any of the other Templar secrets. Since no one on the outside of the group knew what was going on, imagination could run wild.

The troubles of the Templars, however, were still in the future. For many years after their founding, the Templars were regarded as holy men, or monks. Monks also lived in groups, and took vows of poverty and obedience. They, too, swore never to marry. But the Templars were monks with a difference. While most monks did not carry arms, and could not fight, the Templars' main job was fighting. And they fought very well.

Before the founding of the Templars, Christian crusaders had captured Jerusalem and other parts of the Holy Land from the Moslems. Still, the Christian lands were surrounded by hostile Moslems. New Crusades were launched to help secure the Christian lands. These Crusades were failures. Of all the soldiers who went, only the Templars really fought well. For years the Templars were the main support for Christians in the Holy Land. For that reason the Church showered privileges on them.

The Templars did not live only in the Holy

Templar castle in the Holy Land

Land. Their well-fortified headquarters, or Temples, were found in London and Paris and other parts of Europe. Because of their wealth they became bankers. They even loaned money to kings.

By the end of the thirteenth century the Christians were driven out of the Holy Land. The Templars' stronghold, Castle Pilgrim, was the last pocket of Christian resistance.

The career of the Templars did not end with the fall of the Crusaders' kingdom. The powerful order still had many members, headquarters throughout Europe, and of course its great wealth. The Templars also had many special privileges. So, from being greatly loved and respected, they soon became feared and hated.

There is no doubt that the Templars became both greedy and power-hungry. Then they had the bad luck to run up against a person who was even more greedy and more power-hungry, and far more clever. He was Philip IV, King of France.

Philip had once been a friend of the Templars. They had loaned him money. The Grand Master, Jacques de Molay, had been godfather to one of Philip's children. But with friends like Philip you truly do not need enemies. Philip needed money. He decided that if he could seize the Templars' wealth he could pay his debts.

How was he to carry out this scheme? He knew that if he could get the Church to declare that the Templars were no longer true Christians, the Order would be dissolved. Without the protection of the Church the Templars were doomed. Most of their wealth would then go to the king.

On the morning of October 13, 1307, the king's agents seized 140 Templars, including Grand Master Jacques de Molay. All over France other members of the Order were arrested. The charges against them were that they took part in all sorts of terrible and un-

The execution of the Templars

Christian acts. They were charged with worshipping the Devil and practicing magic.

Because the Templars had always been so secretive, a lot of people believed the charges. A lot of people also owed the Templars money. They knew that if the Order was broken up, they would not have to pay their debts. These people said they believed the charges against the Templars, whether they really believed them or not.

According to legend, King Philip was gored to death by a wild boar after being cursed by Jacques de Molay.

The arrested Templars were tortured, and many of them actually confessed. Among those who confessed was Grand Master Jacques de Molay himself. The knights were used to obeying their leader without question. When he confessed, their spirit was broken.

Still, not all of the knights confessed. Those

who would not were burned alive. Many of those who did confess took back their confessions as soon as they were released from prison. The trials of the Templars dragged on for years.

Was there any truth to these charges? A little perhaps, but not much. Most of the Templars had spent years in the Holy Land. They had many contacts with non-Christians. From them the Templars may have picked up some practices that many Christians would not have thought proper. But most of the charges were sheer nonsense. They were exaggerations and inventions of King Philip and his agents.

In the end, nothing could really be proved against the Templars. But the Pope, under pressure from the King of France, declared that the Order should be dissolved anyway.

The final scene of the tragedy came on March 19, 1314. After nearly seven years of captivity, Jacques de Molay was taken from prison to make a public confession. Instead of confessing as expected, he took back his previous confession. The only thing he had done wrong, he said, was to lie in order to save himself from torture. The Order he had led, he declared, was pure and innocent.

De Molay knew that he had condemned himself to death. But before he was burned, he is reported to have pronounced a curse on the King who had persecuted him and the Pope who had failed to support him. The curse was a simple one; they were both to meet him before God's throne for judgment within the year. The Pope did die within a year. King Philip lived a little longer, about eighteen months.

6

FATAL CURSES

Can a curse really harm a person?

Will someone who has been cursed get sick, or even die?

Surprisingly, many scientists think that the answer to both of these questions is yes. But first the person who has been cursed must really believe that the curse can harm him.

Among many primitive peoples cursing is very common. Magicians or witch doctors are greatly feared. If a magician with a powerful reputation curses someone, that person will become depressed and frightened. He may even stop eating because he is sure he is going to die. If this goes on long enough he will really become sick, and die. Scientists do not know exactly how or why this happens. But it does happen. Doctors know that if a sick person loses his will to live, and believes that he is going to die, he is more likely to die. Our mental and physical states are closely tied together.

It isn't only primitive people who may be killed by curses. There are cases of such deaths in modern societies as well. Even in America today there are people who believe in magic. Little groups here and there practice magic, or try to. Sometimes the aim of this magic is to put a spell on their enemies—to get rid of them. Less than a hundred years ago in France, two magical groups battled it out for

Joseph-Antoine Boullan

years. The fight was known as the Battle of Bewitchment, and it ended in death.

The main character in this odd story was a man named Joseph-Antoine Boullan. Boullan had once been a priest, but because of his opinions and actions he had been thrown out of the Church. Boullan then joined a cult headed by Pierre Vintras. When Vintras died, Boullan announced that he was the new head of the group. Most of the members refused to follow him. Boullan and a few followers then settled in the city of Lyons. His main supporter was his housekeeper, a woman by the name of Julie Thibault.

Visitors were allowed to watch Boullan and his followers go through their rites. These appeared harmless enough. But there were rumors that many other things were done in secret. Just what Boullan and his followers were supposed to be doing is not clear, but it was said to be terrible. His enemies accused him of being a Devil worshiper.

It was a strange group, and it was joined by two strange young men. One was called the Marquis Stanislas de Guaita, the other Oswald Wirth. The pair was known to be interested in magic. Boullan initiated them into the secrets of his group. But de Guaita and Wirth were not followers, they were spies. They had their own ideas about magic, and they hated Boullan.

Julie Thibault

As soon as they learned Boullan's secrets, they rushed back to Paris. There they joined with two other young men interested in magic, Edouard Dubus and Joseph Peladan. The four said they were going to put Boullan "on trial." On May 24, 1887, they found Boullan guilty of being an evil sorcerer, and condemned him.

Later, the four claimed that they only intended to expose Boullan as a fraud and an evil man. Boullan, however, thought they had condemned him to death. He remembered all of the magical spells he had taught de Guaita and Wirth when they had been with him in Lyons. He assumed that they were going to turn the magic against him. So Boullan and Julie Thibault prepared to defend themselves, also by magic. Thus began the Battle of Bewitchment.

For several years Boullan and his enemies in Paris cast spells on one another. One of Boullan's friends, a writer named J. K. Huysmans, described the scene at Boullan's house in a letter:

"The battles have begun again since I last wrote to you. . . . Boullan jumps about like a tiger cat . . . He invokes the aid of St. Michael . . . then standing at his altar, he cries out: 'Strike down Peladan, strike down Peladan, strike down Peladan!' And Madam Thibault, her hands folded on her belly, announces: 'It is done.' "

What effect were all of these spells having?

On some people not very much of an effect at all. Huysmans said he felt strange blasts of cold air on his face. His cat also seemed to be bothered. He told a friend this was "undoubtedly owed to the hatred of Stanislas de Guaita." Huysmans put on a magic robe, drew a magic circle on the floor and burned magic chemicals in his fireplace. While this was going on he also loudly chanted magic words. All of this was supposed to protect him from his enemies.

It all sounds like a bit of a joke. But it didn't turn out that way. Just after New Year's of 1893, Boullan became very depressed. He had dreams that he was going to die. He said a blackbird tapped on his window. This was supposed to be a sure sign of death. Julie Thibault also dreamed of death. On January 2, 1893, Boullan wrote a long gloomy letter to a friend. The next day he was dead. He died suddenly, without warning. Exactly what killed him is unknown.

Boullan's friends were sure that he had been killed by black magic. Huysmans said, "Guaita and Peladan practice black magic every day. Poor Boullan was engaged in perpetual conflict with the evil spirits they continually sent him from Paris . . . It is quite possible that my poor friend Boullan has succumbed to a supremely powerful spell."

De Guaita promptly challenged Huysmans

J. K. Huysmans

and another Boullan friend, Jules Bois, to a nonmagical duel—with pistols. Bois accepted. No one was hurt in the duel. Bois said that the bullet had been magically prevented from leaving his pistol barrel.

Edouard Dubus, one of Boullan's four main enemies, was sent to a mental institution later in 1893. As they took him away, he boasted how he had killed Boullan.

Did black magic kill Joseph-Antoine Boullan? Of course not. But fear of magic may have contributed to his death. He had been afraid for a long time. Just before he died, he seems to have become convinced that he was going to die. Doctors know that in this state of mind individuals are more likely to suffer heart attacks, strokes, or other fatal illnesses.

An even stranger magical death took place in England in 1929. In the early years of the twentieth century there had been a magical group called The Order of the Golden Dawn. The group had once been fairly large, and had some famous people as members. One of them was the Irish poet W. B. Yeats. The purpose of the Golden Dawn was to study magic.

The group's leader was a man named S. L. Mathers. He was not an easy man to get along with. He claimed that he was in contact with superior spiritual beings. Since he was the only one who could contact these superior beings, he wanted everyone to do exactly what he said. But a lot of people refused to follow his orders. So the group split up into many smaller groups. Some of the warring groups cast spells on others. When Mathers died in 1918 a few of his friends said it was due to magic. His doctor said he died of influenza. There was a huge influenza epidemic that year, and many people died.

The magical battles did not end with Mathers' death. His widow Moina tried to continue the organization. She also put curses and magical spells on those who opposed her. One woman claimed that she was constantly being attacked by magical cats sent by Moina Mathers. She said that one morning, "I suddenly saw coming down the stairs towards me a gigantic tabby cat, twice the size of a tiger." She managed to make the cat disappear. Another woman, Netta Fornario, was not as fortunate.

Miss Fornario had been a member of one of the groups while all of this magical fighting was going on. She was a nervous, sensitive person who had never been an important member. Somehow she got the idea that she was being pursued.

In the autumn of 1929 she went to the small island of Iona, off the western coast of Scotland. The island is very remote. It is a good place to hide. She rented a room in a house and stayed inside most of the time. She never told her landlady why she had come to the island, though she dropped hints that it might have something to do with magic.

Miss Fornario had been living quietly for two months. Then one morning she woke up in a panic. She told her landlady that she had to leave at once. She seemed confused, but said that "certain people" were trying to get her. Who those people were and how they were trying to get her, she did not know, or did not say. The landlady told her that there would be no boat from the island for several days. Until then she would just have to stay where she was.

Miss Fornario again shut herself up in her room. Later that day she came out. Her landlady said she now had "a calm look of resignation on her face." She told her landlady that she had changed her mind, and was going to stay. How long? she was asked. She didn't know, perhaps forever.

The next morning Netta Fornario did not come down from her room for breakfast. When her landlady went up to see how she was, she found the room empty. No one saw Miss Fornario go out. She had simply disappeared.

The island was searched, and a few hours later Netta Fornario's body was found near the ruins of an ancient village. She was wearing a black cloak with a hood. It was the kind of cloak that had been used in the old Golden Dawn ceremonies. Around her neck was a thick silver chain. Otherwise, she had nothing on. In her hand she clutched a large knife. She had used the knife to cut the sign of the cross in the earth just before she died. The soles of her feet were badly cut. This indicated that she had run a considerable distance over the rocks. The doctor who examined her body said she had died of heart failure.

Back in London, Netta Fornario's friends were shocked. They did not believe the heart failure explanation. They were sure she had been killed by some kind of magical spell. Most of them blamed Moina Mathers. They said that Miss Fornario's body had been scratched, and that Moina Mathers' magical victims always bore scratch marks. Mrs. Mathers denied the charge. There is no evidence that she had even been angry at Netta Fornario.

Once again, it seems that fear of magic, rather than magic itself, had contributed to a death. Netta Fornario was not a particularly strong or mentally stable person. She must have convinced herself that someone had placed a curse or spell upon her. She tried to hide away on a remote island. But the fear was in her. You can't hide from yourself.

That fatal night she was thrown into a complete panic. She put on her magical robes, and took her magical knife. (A knife is often used in magic ceremonies.) Then she tried to run away. But she found you can't run away from yourself. In the end her heart could take it no longer, and she died.

7

PETER RUGG—
WANDERER

The legend of the eternal wanderer is found in many lands.

There is the tale of the Flying Dutchman. That is the story of the captain and his crew fated to sail for all eternity. It was bad luck for any sailors to see the phantom ship.

Throughout Europe there are tales of the Wild Huntsman. He is a hunter who, because of some crime committed in his life, must ride forever through the forest. A local variation is Herne the Hunter, who is supposed to haunt Windsor Forest, in England. One of the most popular legends of the Middle Ages was the tale of the Wandering Jew. He was supposed to have been a witness to the crucifixion. Because of some insult to Jesus, he was fated to wander the earth till Judgment Day. For hundreds of years people reported that they had actually seen the Wandering Jew.

To be an eternal wanderer has always been considered a terrible curse.

America has its own version of the legend of the wandering man. It was repeated frequently in the Boston area about 150 years ago. The most complete version of the story comes in a letter credited to William Austin. He said he had actually seen the wanderer, and spoken to him.

According to Austin, he first met the wanderer in 1820. He was taking a coach to Bos-

Herne the Hunter

ton. The coach was so crowded that he had to ride up front with the driver.

They had gone about ten miles when Austin noticed that the horses were becoming very nervous. The driver then told him that it was about to rain. Since there was not a cloud in the sky, Austin wondered why he made such a forecast. Because, said the driver, they were about to meet "the storm-breeder." The horses always knew first.

The storm-breeder turned out to be a man driving an open carriage. He drove quickly, always looking nervously from side to side. Inside the carriage sat a small child, a girl. The traveler seemed to be perpetually followed by

The Wandering Jew

rain clouds. After he passed, the rain ended, and the horses calmed down.

The driver of the coach told Austin that he had seen the man and child many times before. Often the man had stopped him and asked the way to Boston. But even if the man was going in the opposite direction, he would not take any advice. The coach driver simply refused to talk to him anymore. He had no idea who the man was. The man never stopped except to ask the way to Boston, and insisted that he must reach there that very night.

Austin had nearly forgotten about the strange incident. Then, three years later, he happened to be staying at a hotel in Hartford, Connecticut. He was standing on the front step of the hotel when he heard a man say, "Here comes Peter Rugg and his child! He looks wet and weary, and farther from Boston than ever." Down the road Austin saw the same carriage and same storm cloud he had met on the road to Boston. The carriage was heading for the hotel.

The stranger told Austin that he had seen Peter Rugg twenty years earlier. He had been asked the way to Boston. When he was told he was going in the wrong direction and must turn back, Rugg had replied:

"Alas! It is all turn back! Boston shifts with the wind and plays all around the compass. One man tells me it is to the east, another to the

View of Boston in 1816

west, and the guideposts, too, all point the wrong way."

As Peter Rugg neared the hotel, Austin decided to speak to him. He stepped out into the street and waved down the carriage.

"Are you Peter Rugg?" he asked.

"My name is Peter Rugg," said the man. "I have unfortunately lost my way. I am wet and weary. Will you please direct me to Boston?"

"You live in Boston? On what street?"

"On Middle Street."

"When did you leave Boston?"

"I don't know exactly. It must have been some time ago."

"But how did you and your child get so wet? It has not rained here today."

A street in Boston in the early 1800s

"There has been a heavy shower up the river. But I shall not reach Boston tonight if I tarry. Which road do I take to Boston?"

Rugg was then told that he was over 100 miles from Boston, in Connecticut. But he refused to believe this. He insisted that he was forty miles or less from Boston, and drove off rapidly.

Austin now thought he had a clue to the puzzle. He decided that next time he was in Boston he would try to find out more about the mysterious traveler.

75

Austin went to Boston and found a Mrs. Croft, an old lady who had lived on Middle Street for many years. The woman told him that just a few months earlier she had actually been visited by Peter Rugg.

Just at twilight he had come to the door and asked for a Mrs. Rugg. He was told that Mrs. Rugg had once lived in the house but had died twenty years ago. And she had been quite old when she died.

Peter Rugg insisted that this must be a mistake. He asked all sorts of questions which indicated he knew nothing of how Boston had grown or changed. Finally, he decided that he was not really in Boston. His horse became impatient and began pawing the street. Rugg went away muttering, "No home tonight."

Austin wished to know more, but Mrs. Croft could add nothing. She directed him to the house of James Felt. Felt was over eighty, and had lived in the same house for fifty years. Felt knew the story of Peter Rugg. He had heard it from his grandfather.

In about 1770 a man named Peter Rugg had lived on Middle Street. He was a man of fierce temper, who would take advice from no one.

One autumn morning Rugg took his little daughter for a drive to the town of Concord. On the way back there was a violent storm. He stopped at the house of a friend who asked him to stay the night. "Let the storm increase," swore Rugg. "I will see home tonight in spite of the storm, or may I never see home!"

With these words, he whipped his horse and disappeared into the night. He did not get home that night, or the next, or any other night. No trace of him or his daughter was ever found. And there was no clue to what happened to them.

8

FATAL TWENTY

The most famous curse in America today is called Fatal Twenty. It is about the presidents of the United States.

Many U.S. presidents have either died in office or, sadly, been assassinated. The remarkable fact is that practically all who died in office were elected within a twenty-year cycle. Here is the record:

William Henry Harrison was elected in 1840. He died of pneumonia after serving in office for only a month. He was the first U.S. president to die in office.

Abraham Lincoln was elected twenty years later, in 1860. As we all know, he was assassinated by John Wilkes Booth.

James A. Garfield was elected president in 1880. Four months after his inauguration he was shot by Charles Guiteau. Garfield clung to life for a few months, but finally died from his wounds on September 19, 1881.

William McKinley was the winner of the 1900 election. The following year he was shot to death by Leon Czolgosz.

Warren G. Harding was elected in 1920. He died suddenly while on a speaking tour in 1923.

Franklin D. Roosevelt was elected in 1940. He also died in office.

The most recent "victim" of the Fatal Twenty curse was John F. Kennedy. He was elected president in 1960 and assassinated in Dallas in 1963.

William Henry
Harrison, elected
1840, died in office

Abraham Lincoln,
elected 1860,
assassinated

James A. Garfield,
elected 1880,
assassinated

William McKinley,
elected 1900,
assassinated

Warren G. Harding,
elected 1920,
died in office

Franklin D. Roosevelt,
elected 1940,
died in office

John F. Kennedy,
elected 1960,
assassinated

There was only one president who died in office, but was not elected in this twenty-year cycle. He was Zachary Taylor. Taylor was elected in 1848. He died in 1850. The only two presidents who were elected in this twenty-year cycle who did not die in office were Thomas Jefferson, elected in 1800, and James Monroe, elected in 1820. The Fatal Twenty legend holds that the cycle did not begin until 1840—that is, with the election of William Henry Harrison.

When you first read over the list of deaths and assassinations it looks very impressive. But, actually, to make it all work out correctly, you have to do a little juggling. Here's how:

The cycle works for President Harrison, who was elected for the first time in 1840 and died during his first term.

It does not quite work for President Lincoln. He was elected to his first term in 1860. He was assassinated at the start of his *second* term.

President Garfield, who was elected in 1880, was assassinated during his first term, so the cycle works for him.

President McKinley presents even a greater problem than Lincoln. He was first elected president in 1896. He got into the twenty-year cycle only because he was *re-elected* in 1900. He was assassinated during his second term.

Warren Harding fits the cycle neatly. He was elected in 1920 and died during his first term.

The greatest problem to the cycle is Franklin D. Roosevelt. Roosevelt was elected president four times. He was first elected president in 1932. He does not get into the cycle until he was elected to his *third* term in 1940. He died in office at the beginning of his *fourth* term, in 1945.

Like Harrison, Garfield, and Harding, John F. Kennedy fits neatly into the cycle. He was elected in 1960 and assassinated during his first term.

Beliefs about certain numbers being fatal or unlucky have been around a long time. The British have quite a number of them about their own kings and queens. Here is one of them. The number 88 was supposed to be very unlucky for the Stuart royal family. They were first kings of Scotland and then of Scotland and England.

Robert II, the first Stuart king, died in 1388.

James II of Scotland was killed in battle in 1488.

Mary Stuart was beheaded in 1588.

James II of England was dethroned in 1688.

The last Stuart claimant to the English throne, Charles Edward, died in 1788.

The man who dethroned James II was Oliver Cromwell. For him, the date September 3 seems to have been important. He was born on September 3, 1599. He won a critical battle on September 3, 1650. On September 3, the following year, he won another critical battle. He died September 3, 1658.

Some sort of cycles can be worked out for the kings of France and Spain and elsewhere. Most statisticians—that is, people who work with numbers—say that such cycles are just coincidence. If you have many numbers to play with, you can work out a cycle or a series of matching numbers if you try hard enough.

An extraordinarily large number of British kings seem to have died on a Saturday. Both the great English writer Shakespeare and the great Spanish writer Cervantes died on April

Mary Stuart on her way to her execution. The number 88 was unlucky for her family.

23, 1616. The most amazing coincidence of American history is that John Adams, the second president of the United States, and Thomas Jefferson, the third president, both died on the same day. And that day was July 4, 1826. July 4, the date of the Declaration of Independence, which Jefferson wrote and Adams signed, is considered the most significant document in American history.

The assassination of John F. Kennedy brought out all sorts of numerical comparisons, particularly comparisons between the Kennedy and Lincoln assassinations. The names of both murdered presidents contain seven letters. The names of Kennedy's accused assassin, Lee Harvey Oswald, and Lincoln's assassin, John Wilkes Booth, both have fifteen letters.

Is there some hidden significance in all of this? Well, perhaps, but as with the Fatal Twenty cycle, the comparison is not as neat as it first appears to be. We used only the last names of the presidents, but the full names of the assassins. If we change things around the comparison doesn't work at all. The name John Fitzgerald Kennedy has 21 letters, while the name Abraham Lincoln only has 14. There are 6 letters in the name Oswald and 5 in Booth.

But people who believe that the Lincoln and Kennedy assassinations are linked by some kind of unknown fate are not easily discouraged. They will point out to you that Lincoln was shot in the Ford Theatre, and when Kennedy was shot he was riding in a Lincoln automobile made by the Ford Motor Company.

As for the Fatal Twenty cycle, whether people will continue to believe in it or not depends on the fate of the president elected in 1980.

88

9

THE CURSE OF THE
THREE SISTERS

A lot of places on earth are rumored to be cursed. But usually we think that such places are tombs, or pyramids, or castles. They are places exotic and faraway. But one of the most powerful curses is said to be centered on a place which is neither exotic nor faraway. It is centered on three large boulders in the Potomac River, near Washington, D.C. They can be seen quite clearly if you drive along the George Washington Parkway, on the Virginia side of the river.

The curse itself is supposed to go back to Indian times. But it is said to have been powerful enough to stop the construction of a modern bridge.

The three large granite rocks are called the Three Sisters. According to the legend, the curse of the Three Sisters began long before Europeans had settled the region.

The land along the Potomac was rich in resources. There was plenty of game in the woods and plenty of fish in the river. Wild berries, nuts, and seeds abounded. The land was fertile, and corn, beans, and squash grew well there.

Naturally, many Indian tribes were attracted to such an area. Indian settlements ranged up and down the river. But the different tribes were not always at peace with one another. A particularly fierce rivalry raged between the Susquehannocks from the north and the Powhatans from the south.

During one battle a village of Powhatans was trapped by a large party of Susquehannocks. The Powhatan village was well protected by a palisade—a wooden fence made of sharp stakes. It would have been too costly in lives for the Susquehannocks to try to get into the village. On the other hand, it was very risky for the Powhatans to try and get out. Finally, the village ran out of food. Some of the old and the weak had already died from starvation. Even the strong young warriors were growing weak from hunger. That was what the Susquehannocks had counted on. Soon, they thought, they could take the village without a fight.

The chief of the village was desperate. He decided he must take some of his strongest men into the forest to hunt for food. It was a dangerous move. They might all be killed, but it was better than waiting to starve to death. The chief had three young sons. They wanted to go on the hunt, but he would not let them. He said they were too young. Besides, they were needed to defend the village while the warriors were gone.

The boys were bitterly disappointed. They wanted to prove to their father and to the other members of their tribe that they were men. They had a plan. They were going to creep out of the village at dawn and catch enough fresh

The Three Sisters Rocks

An Indian village surrounded by a palisade

Indians fishing

fish to feed the women, children, and old men until the hunting party returned.

All but one of the village's canoes had been destroyed by the Susquehannocks. The chief's sons had hidden it. At dawn they slipped the canoe from its hiding place and paddled across the river before the fog burned off.

Unfortunately, they were spotted by an enemy scouting party. They were captured, and put to death in full view of those who had remained in the village.

Among those who watched were the three daughters of the tribe's powerful medicine man. They had loved the three slain braves. Now they vowed revenge. They decided to cross the river and persuade the rival chief to give them the warriors who had killed their lovers. The three maidens counted on their own beauty and the power of their father's magic to accomplish this seemingly hopeless task.

They had no canoe, so they tied several logs together to form a raft. Before anyone else could notice they boarded their raft and pushed off into the river.

The currents and the winds were too strong for the raft. The three sisters were carried downstream, toward the open sea. They might have been able to save themselves, but they would not be able to cross the river.

The three sisters joined arms and pronounced a curse. If they—the daughters of a powerful medicine man—could not cross the river, then no one would cross at that point again. *Ever*.

To seal the curse the three sisters jumped into the river and drowned.

Then according to the legend, a tremendous storm broke over the Potomac. Lightning struck the river where the three Indian maidens had died. The storm whipped the waters into a white-capped frenzy.

By morning the storm had ended. There appeared in the river, at the point where the three sisters had drowned, three huge granite boulders that had not been there before. They are still there.

The curse of the Three Sisters was known to some of the earliest Europeans who came to the area. Captain John Smith wrote in his diary about the curse. He also said that he heard sounds of moaning and sobbing coming from near the Three Sisters Rocks.

Old rivermen claim that the same moaning and sobbing sounds will be heard before the curse claims another victim. And there have been plenty of victims—fishermen, swimmers, and canoeists who try to cross the river near the rocks have died.

But perhaps the ancient curse's most spectacular victim was a bridge. There was a plan to build a bridge across the Potomac near the rocks. It was to be called the Three Sisters Bridge. There were many who didn't want the bridge, for a variety of reasons. They had taken the plan to court. But those who wanted the bridge were only slowed, not stopped. By 1972 they had actually begun work on the bridge.

Then suddenly a violent storm struck. The waters of the Potomac were once again whipped into a frenzy. It was said that bolts of lightning struck the waters near the Three Sisters Rocks, just as they had in the legend. It was one of the worst storms in Washington history. Flooding swept away the work that had been done on the Three Sisters Bridge.

Since that time, the plan to build a Three Sisters Bridge has not been brought up again.

10

NONE SHALL
KNOW YOUR
GRAVE

During the early years of this century Horatio Herbert Kitchener was the most famous soldier in Britain. He was a stern-looking man with a bushy mustache. He was the perfect picture of a military man.

When World War I broke out, no one in England could escape his face. It stared at them from hundreds of thousands of recruiting posters. There was Kitchener pointing a finger at you. The slogan read, "Your Country Needs YOU!" The campaign was so successful that when the United States entered the war, we adopted it. Instead of Kitchener, the U.S. posters used Uncle Sam.

Kitchener had come from an army family. Until he was nearly fifty he had a successful but unspectacular army career. He was known to be cold, and unemotional, not the sort to panic under fire. However, he was not well liked by his fellow officers. He was too cold, and a little bit ruthless and brutal, to boot.

But he knew Arabic and he knew Africa. So in 1898 Kitchener was chosen to avenge the worst military defeat Britain had suffered in its recent history.

Some thirteen years earlier there had been a revolt against the British in the Sudan. The leader of the revolt was called the Mahdi— "the Chosen One." He said he had been chosen by God to drive the British out of the land.

Lord Kitchener on World War I recruiting poster

American version of the Kitchener recruiting poster

The Mahdi's troops had taken the city of Khartoum and killed General George Gordon, the British commander. Gordon had been a hero in Britain. His death came as a great shock.

Kitchener led the army that was to retake Khartoum. It turned out to be an easy victory. The British had modern weapons. Their enemies did not. Kitchener had wished to capture the Mahdi himself. But he was too late. The leader had died several years earlier.

Kitchener wanted some personal revenge. His troops destroyed the Mahdi's tomb. The leader's remains were taken out and thrown into the Nile River. Kitchener kept the Mahdi's skull. First, he said he was going to use it as an inkstand. In the end, he simply sent it to Cairo as a trophy of war.

As the victorious Kitchener was riding through the streets of Khartoum a ragged man stepped out of the crowd and shouted a curse. "As you threw our holy leader's remains into the water, so will your body be swallowed by water. You will drown like a dog, and none shall know your grave."

Kitchener was reported to have repeated the story several times. It didn't seem to bother him. In fact, he actually enjoyed the possibility that he had been cursed.

If there was a curse, it certainly didn't hurt his career. He led several other successful engagements. Honors were heaped upon him. He was made Lord Kitchener and given the highest rank in the British Army, that of Field Marshal.

When World War I broke out, Lord Kitchener was appointed Secretary of State for War. The British public was wildly happy about the appointment. They thought the hero of Khartoum would solve the problems of the British Army. He didn't. In fact, as Secretary of State for War, Lord Kitchener was a disaster.

He was completely out of touch with the sort of war that was being fought. He didn't believe in steel helmets and tanks. All modern innovations had to be adopted over his objections. That meant delay after delay. Everybody in the government agreed that Lord Kitchener had to go. But how to get rid of him? He was so popular that if he was dismissed by the government, then the government would promptly be dismissed by the voters.

Then someone—no one seems to know who—got the idea to sending Kitchener to Russia for a week. Russia was Britain's ally in the war. Russia's army was on the verge of collapse. Just what the hero of the desert was supposed to do in the snows of Russia was never clear. He knew absolutely nothing about Russia.

Yet Kitchener gladly agreed to go. Perhaps he just wanted to get away from all the fighting

Lord Kitchener

in the government. Perhaps he really thought he could help Russia.

The problem was getting Lord Kitchener all the way to Russia. Flying was out of the question. The airplanes of the day could not make such a flight. The seas were patrolled by German submarines, and filled with enemy mines. A sea journey would be dangerous, but it was the only way.

It was decided to send Kitchener on the light cruiser *Hampshire*. The route chosen was one regularly patrolled for submarines and swept for mines. At the last minute, however, a sudden storm caused a change of plans. The new route was also considered relatively safe, but it had not been swept for mines.

At 4:45 P.M. on June 5, 1916, the *Hampshire* with Lord Kitchener aboard steamed out of a Scottish naval base. Three hours later she blew up. British soldiers on the coast of Scotland witnessed the explosion.

Rescue craft were sent out immediately. But the ship had sunk so quickly, and the water was so rough and so cold, that there were only eleven survivors. Lord Kitchener was not among them. Nor was his body ever located.

There were all sorts of questions about his death. If the *Hampshire* had struck a German mine, as the government said, how was it possible that enemy minelayers had been able to operate in sight of the coast? But a war was raging. All questions were silenced "for security reasons."

The British public was shocked and saddened by the death of their hero. High officials were not so unhappy at the loss. With Kitchener gone, they thought the war effort would go more smoothly.

After the war some of the questions about Kitchener's death were answered. The mine that sank the *Hampshire* was put down by an advanced type of submarine. That is why it had not been seen from the coast. Before that, mines had to be laid by surface craft.

But why had the Germans mined that particular area? Had they known about Lord Kitchener's trip? There were all sorts of rumors, but nothing was ever proved.

There was even a story that German agents had been aboard the *Hampshire,* and that Lord Kitchener had not been killed in the blast. According to this story, he had made it to shore with several other survivors. One of them was a German agent. This agent then killed him and threw his body into the sea. The body was then swept by currents all the way to Norway. It was found by fishermen, and buried in an unmarked grave.

This particular story attracted a great deal of attention for several months. The man who promoted the tale said he had actually found Kitchener's corpse in Norway and brought it back to England. But when the coffin was opened it was found to be empty.

Generally, the story was regarded to be a hoax.

Today there is an impressive tomb to Lord Kitchener in St. Paul's Cathedral in London. The tomb is empty. And some people recall a curse pronounced many years before in Khartoum. The curse warned of a watery death and ended: ". . . and none shall know your grave."

11

THE FINAL CURSE

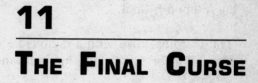

In this book we have read about a large number of curses, some quite terrible. I thought we might end with one of the most complete curses ever written. It comes from an old book called *Ingoldsby Legends*. It is in the form of a poem about a high Church official who places a curse upon a thief.

The Cardinal rose with a dignified look,
He call'd for his candle, his bell, and his
   book!
In holy anger, and pious grief,
He solemnly cursed that rascally thief!
He cursed him at board, he cursed him in
   bed;
From the sole of his foot to the crown of
   his head;
He cursed him in sleeping, that every
   night
He should dream of the devil, and wake
   in a fright;
He cursed him in living, he cursed him in
   drinking,
He cursed him in coughing, in sneezing,
   in winking;
He cursed him in sitting, in standing, in
   lying;
He cursed him in walking, in riding, in
   flying,

The Final Curse

He cursed him living, he cursed him
   dying—
Never was heard such a terrible curse!
But what gave rise to no little surprise,
Nobody seem'd one penny the worse!

INDEX

Index

Index

ABOUT THE AUTHOR

DANIEL COHEN is the author of many books for both young readers and adults, and he is a former managing editor of *Science Digest* magazine. His titles include *Supermonsters, The Greatest Monsters in the World, Real Ghosts, Creatures from UFO's, The World's Most Famous Ghosts, The Monsters of Star Trek,* and *Missing! Stories of Strange Disappearances,* all of which are available in Archway Paperback editions.

Mr. Cohen was born in Chicago and has a degree in journalism from the University of Illinois. He appears frequently on radio and television and has lectured at colleges and universities throughout the country. He lives with his wife, young daughter, two dogs and three cats in Port Jervis, New York.